Wavelengths

2011 Savant Anthology of Poetry

Edited by
Zachary M. Oliver

Savant Books
Honolulu, HI, USA
2011

Published in the USA by Savant Books and Publications
2630 Kapiolani Blvd #1601
Honolulu, HI 96826
http://www.SavantBooksAndPublications.com

Printed in the USA

Edited by Zachary M. Oliver
Cover Photos and Design by Daniel S. Janik

13-digit ISBN: 978-0-9829987-6-2
10 digit ISBN: 0-9829987-6-7

Dedication

Poetry is a mystical communication of the inspired moments of our lives.

In these pages, words are tightly packed in rhythmic lines and enriched with meaning and symbolism. Some are playful, some terrifying, some sensual: All are deeply human. And so, I dedicate this little anthology to our great benefactor, a lover of this eye-blink life, and one of the greatest human beings I've ever known: Daniel S. Janik.

We all thank you for breathing life into Savant and for sharing this forum to artists, both budding and arrived.

- Zachary M. Oliver

Table of Contents

Alex Kelley is a writer who specializes in poetry and select monologues and dialogues. Born in 1986, he has been writing for the past 10 years, and is currently living in Georgia.

No One's Home
Alex Kelley

My patience and I are walking through an empty house,
Old dusty floors, oil-deprived doors,
And every step I take, decides to make a sound,
And it reminds me of the life, I used to have.
I walk up these stairs,
down I fell when I was nine,
That hole's still in the corner,
that I made a year later,
I walk down the upstairs hall,
and look at spots and stains,
In the bathroom, a crack from a pipe burst,
When I put Daddy's keys down the drain.
Now I stand here in my sister's room,
Where I was told to stay away,
But my sister's not here,
So I walk in and out, rebellion prevails.
I see myself in my room, running all over the place,
Jumping on the bed, getting older as I blink,
The marks are still on the wall, see how I've grown,
And my handy lock is still there, for when I wanted to be
alone.
Chilling out in the space where my bed used to be,
Looking out the door, and across the hall,
Into that infamous lair I called my parents' room,
And to this day I dare not go.
I walked back out that door that started it all,
Dead lawn, rusted knobs, broken windows,
Faded paint, the feel of age,
I step away, and let history sleep.

Daniel S. Janik is a mult-award-winning poet with works appearing in seventeen books throughout the world. Author of "Footprints, Smiles and Little White Lies" (Savant 2008), "The Illustrated Middle Earth" (Savant 2008) and "Last and Final Harvest" (Savant 2008), his poems most recently appeared in "First Breath—2010 Savant Anthology of Poetry" (Savant 2011). He has penned over 60 books and publications under his legal name, including "Unlock the Genius Within" (Rowman and Littlefield 2005), "How to Choose the Best English Language School in the USA" (AuthorHouse 2005), "Sourdough Scott's Bedtime Fairy Tales from Alaska" (Publication Consultants 2006), and "A Whale's Tale" (Savant 2009) and numerous other works under various pen names including Gary Martine and Raymond Gaynor.

More Mine, Complete

Daniel S. Janik

The eye of my pen
Through ages past and present
Has scourged and burned
What little there is left in reality to see
So, tonight, it rests in the present
The happiness of being alive.
Gone, the objectiveness
That science and reason use as their tools of conquest.
Tonight, I revel in subjectiveness
Responding reflexively to the faint beats of my heart's
desire,
And wade, bare foot, through the ponds of illiteracy
continually surrounding me.
If, seeing me, you cannot speak, then it is only
The more yours complete.
There is no loss of feeling in simply being,
But rather a joy unspoken
Only felt deep in the guts
Then locked forever away.
I, too, once kept a star from my midnight mind
In my pocket to show to inquisitive strangers.
My, how it shone, like a new penny,
Or maybe it was a new penny that shone like a star.
I showed it to everyone who would pause long enough to
look
It was my happiness and
Joy
I cannot express it
And so, it is more mine, complete.

Born in Europe, IKO traveled westward towards a warm and wonderful climate. She has been a university and college instructor of foreign languages, an entrepreneur, a translator (French, German, and English), and an artist. When not spending her time pursuing an active outdoor lifestyle, IKO reads copiously, especially in her areas of interest: philosophy (both Eastern and Western traditions) and the many fascinating religious traditions of our world. Balancing this combination of active and esoteric, IKO believes that the ambiance of Hawaii corresponds to the harmony of her family life.

Personal Quest
IKO

In my own world
I want to grow—
ineffable—
Unleash the powers lent to me—
indomitable—
Surging forth
Jutting out
Choking me

Give me space
Let me breathe—I have to grow!

Jean Yamasaki Toyama is a poet, scholar, translator and writer of fiction. She is emerita professor of French at the University of Hawai'i at Mânoa, where she taught and was associate dean of the College of Languages, Linguistics and Literature. She lives in Hawai'i where she was born and raised.

To Poets of Destitute Times
Jean Yamasaki Toyama

A destitute poet
le voilà
in a comfortable chair
behind inches of glass
martini in hand
safe from the frothing destruction
safe from the vertiginous swirl
of gushing blood
crying babes
orphaned on the 56 inch screen.

"I drink to you,
suicide bombers, sharp shooters, soldiers of all
persuasions:
Palestinians, Israelis, Sunnis, Shiites, Afghanis
you know, assorted patriot-terrorists

I lift my glass to all
armed and ready to die
for freedom
for justice
(no doubt worthy causes).

I toast those with conviction to kill
sweet little girls and tired old women,
disembowel plump newborns with jagged machetes
or fragmenting bombs."

Their truth enthralls their partisans,
these poets of blood.

Their righteousness leaves me dumb
Their certitude inspires my thirst.

Michael Shorbis a poet, technical writer, editor and children's book author who lives in San Francisco. He writes frequently about environmental issues and historical topics. His work has appeared in over one hundred publications, including MICHIGAN QUARTERLY, KANSAS QUARTERLY, THE NATION, COMMONWEAL, RATTLE, THE SUN, SALZBURG POETRY REVIEW, EUROPEAN JUDAISM, QUEEN'S QUARTERLY and THE SHAKESPEARE NEWSLETTER.

Dedication

An attempt to express the bond we feel with the victims of the earthquake in Haiti.

Haitian Earthquake
Michael Shorb

A portion of the over-
extracted and parching
earth revolts, claws
deep enough into stone
to launch a sixty second
spasm of violent shaking,
and all in the human camp
feel the same blood chill
of recognition:

How close to ants
we are, dragging and crawling
through rubble, digging
desperately into dirt,
searching for extended hands,
seeking to recover the lost
voices of loved ones,
listening for the muted
cries of the vanishing,
the mumbled prayers,
the incomprehensible whispers.

On Fire
Alex Kelley

In this maze, there's a feeling,
Describable, and yet, not at all,
Hour hands continue to fall,
And there's smoke coming through the walls,
It's not Hell—too simple,
It's not a house—too complicated,
But somewhere on this earth, the world is aflame,
I feel heat, I feel sensitivity, I feel rage, I feel fear,
I haven't moved an inch, but I've aged a year,
And it's only getting hotter, it's only getting worse,
Or is it getting better? Too lost to know.
In this haze, there's a sight,
Oranges, yellow, and reds—even whites,
Flickering violently as it gives off its light,
Like a wounded soldier who set off the flare,
Calling for help as it cries in the air,
Making me sweat as the heat gives its glare,
The hottest glance, the nastiest stare,
And to know what side it's on,
Is as good as flipping a coin,
On one side it'll give you warmth and shelter,
While another side will ruin your life.
In this blaze, something's burning,
And even though the walls are now ignited,
There's not a dark mark on them to be found,
So who's the victim of this cinder love affair?
Is it me? Surrounded with no way out of this heated
prison,
Or is it fire itself, who doesn't know it now,
But is just as trapped as I was,

In this decaying flood, clouded by ash and black air,
Yet, somehow, I make it out of this calm insanity,
But I refuse to leave entirely...
For it's cold outside...

Helen Doan is a Vietnamese-American writer born in Kien Giang, Vietnam in 1981 and came to San Jose, California in 1986 where she grew up. Doan moved from the Bay Area to Southern California in 2002 where she spent over seven years writing feature-length screenplays and keeping a diary of her independence. Currently residing in New York City, she anticipates the publication of her candid memoir "On My Behalf" by Savant Books and Publications.

Pretentious Hearth
Helen Doan

There, a burst of moonlight
A friendly, golden glint
Keeping homes aglow at night
With its soft and mild tint

Its deceiving feel, pretentious hearth
Its regality, in passing
Tried to sell its glow for warmth
Its glory, everlasting

Wavelengths

Deceived

Helen Doan

I was his one and only
A beloved and deceived
One who took too well upon me
To wear it on my sleeve

The beauty of a laugh line
The timelessness of tears
Housing this young heart of mine
That knew but never feared

For the tenderness he gave
Conquered mountains, parted seas
Offering every dream engraved
Promised then denied to me

Wavelengths

Mai Poina

Jean Yamasaki Toyama

I remember
Lili'uokalani, on that raging January day.
"All right . . . I will go," you said.
Then exiled in your very own room,
a prisoner in your very own home,
you wrote songs we sing today.

I remember
Lili'uokalani,
heart burning like Pele's mountain
at the wrong with no peaceful
way to right.

I think of you,
Lili'uokalani, and of your people,
the *kanaka maoli*,
and of your uprightness towards us
of different colors,
born here and
come from other places.
We, too, seek right for wrong.

Mai nânâ 'ino 'ino
Nâ hewa o kânaka,
Akâ, e huikala,
A ma'ema'e nô.

"Oh! look not on their failings,
Nor on the sins of men
Forgive with loving kindness,

21

That we might be made pure."

May all our hearts be made pure,
Lili'uokalani,
Queen Lili'uokalani.

Jeremiah Daniel Ussher enjoys a life with his wife and two sons. He is a Musician and Poet currently disguised as a Contractor. Appreciating every moment shared with his family he strives to make the most of this of a wonderful life that he has been given.

Zachary Oliver EdD continually searches for his niche in life. He believes in living life always prepared to learn and share. Basking the beautiful sunshine and cool trade winds, he shares his life with his beautiful ohana and awesome students. Currently authoring a book, he is sketching some ideas about learning and coloring these ideas with vibrant stories about his decade in the classroom.

Song of a Family Man
Jeremy Ussher and Zachary Oliver

I am poetic discovery at its most basic, undying, and ever-forging stratum.

In my youth, I seized opportunities, crammed these moments full of will, and ran head-first into stone walls leaving cold, hard, stinging regret throbbing at my brow.

Yet, I am thankful for this life, these breaths, and the lessons living in every moment.

I have found love in a woman, the most perfect of creations. Beyond beautiful, her soul exudes virtue and light into a world which seems to have these qualities in short supply.

Together, we have made children. Ever-constant, ever-evolving, and ever-individual; an energy animates each of them. Each new action they display awes me.

An artist of words and ideas, a musician of time and key, I am, most of all, a happy man. Creation pours forth from me; I am genesis.

Light has only now come into being. This sun is only casting the first rays of a promising day.

No longer searching for certainty in a world undefined; I find solid foundations waiting for me.

Vivekanand Jha is a poet, translator and research scholar from Darbhanga, Bihar, India. He has a Diploma in Electronics, Certificate in Computer Hardware and Networking, an MA in English, and is also earning his Ph. D. on the poetry of the noted Indian English poet Jayanta Mahapatra from Lalit Narayan Mithila University Darbhanga. He is son of noted professor, poet and award winning translator Dr. Rajanand Jha (Crowned with Sahitya Akademi Award, New Delhi). He is the author of five books of poetry: <u>Hands Heave to Harm and Hamper</u>, <u>Spam: A Satire on E-Sex</u>, <u>Songs of Innocence and Adolescence</u>, <u>My Poems Falter and Fall</u>, and <u>Time Moves Clockwise Only</u>. His works have been widely published in magazines round the world.

Humanity Died
Vivekanand Jha

There was a gathering on the mid road
I have also excited to join them
Expecting some interesting things to see
I found humanity has met with an accident
It bleeds and cries in pain
And seeks some solace from onlookers
Who called themselves
Wonderful and beautiful creatures of the world.

We remain mute spectators
As if it were a scene of movie.
None of hands heave to help him:
In some they were blinking like a cursor
In some they were like a flip-flop
In some they try to reach
But their deaf and stony emotion
Fail to respond.

But the heart of Atropos in heaven
Melt as He listened the pain and moaning
Of the humanity and He extended His hands
To support and succour
And we found humanity died.

Erin L George is a freelance writer from Southern New Hampshire. George has had several poems and articles published in journals, anthologies and magazines since 1995, including Behavioral Healthcare Magazine. She has received numerous awards from the New England Press Association for her work as a journalist. She recently self-published a book of poetry, Dandelion Dance, and is currently working on a second, Insideout.

Kristopher
Erin L George

I offer you back to the waves, my son,
where you bathe in your father's eyes -
a man too blind to see.

I see it, the twirls and hunger
of the ocean. Remembering how he held me -
strong and never blinking.

Your three-year-old giggles whisper
of our love. Perfect seashells bobbing
to shore, unafraid of high tide.

It once sat in his drawer, wet on my scent -
tucked between his shorts. He took it out,
as I do you, to smell.

I inhale you. His soap and salty sweat
no different. Your stocky build mocking
the frailty of his courage.

I offer you to the moon, my son,
where we made love on wicker chairs
and slept in a hammock.

I see it, twisting under fireworks
on a Fourth of July while she worked -
unaware as he made promises.

Our six-month-old love affair
hanging in the summer heat, cooled in compare

to his kisses and lies.

But do not fear, my son. I've always been one
for ocean swimming. Never afraid of sharks
or jellyfish stings.

You take my eyes, my dear,
and look wide into the sea. Knowing of perfect
seashells and promises kept.

I release you to the stars, my boy,
where you shall throw back a comet
he'll never catch. And know I'm there:

Open hearted, like the great ocean, wide
and yawning big on your love. While he sits
on a shore, drunk on a lie.

So take my heart, my son,
and let it take you places he'd never dream -
swimming strong in his absence.

You'll offer him the waves one day
and he won't recognize your strength -
perfect as a seashell: perfectly complete.

Beware, my son! He'll say it was insanity
and I a mere phase. Like a lovesick tide on eclipse
or a hermit crab set free.

He'll tell you he did not know;
his words are empty shells. Not all men, my K,
are made the same.

All I ask of you, my son, is to take this away:
Grow to be a better man. Ride upon the wave.
Keep your promises and stay brave.

Cara Richardson (born 17 August 1990) is a student studying Diagnostic Radiography at St. Georges University of London who likes to write in her spare time. Author's note: "I'm not sure this is the kind of poem that's usually published or the type you're looking for, but I hope you like it."

Poem 1

Cara Richardson

I'm shy even though I'm a show off.
I'm mean even though I love you.
I'm insecure, but it is not that obvious:
I need you.
Surprisingly, I do not feel jealous or envious.
I am true and honest.
Everyday, I want to change something, become someone.
There is so much to do, to create, to be:
so many questions with no answers!
I'm not diplomatic, just curious.
My friends make me feel strong, without them I'd be
empty.
They are my happiness, my will power, my energy.
I want to do good, but I guess I must be vain. For my own
success,
all I know is, if I truly love you, I will be there for you for
life.

Wavelengths

Hard Times

Daniel S. Janik

Hard times
We spread, instead of butter
On our breadcrusts.
Worry,
The bitter hops we drink
To wash away the aftertaste.
With steel umbilici
Concrete placentae
The new world bears her young.
Discontent
We remember
Instead of flowers,
The dirtied, vacant faces
The steaming feces left behind by slain warrior-men
We remember
Instead of love.
Oh my children!
Where is your place
In a world
Of green, electric blood?

Bully-Free Zone
Zachary M. Oliver

The air at recess was filled with
a hundred glorious goofs,
giggles, and
games.

Then, the siren sounded.

With a single
blast, the children sat. Little faces frozen in the
shadow of a
classroom.

A trembling quiet curled.

Dominating the moment from its vantage on a
door, a bright and bold poster
prominantly declared this place a
"Bully-Free Zone."

Wavelengths

The Face

Helen Doan

Heads misplaced, thoughts erased
Gone to its eternal doom
Recall a time, forget the face
That sought but never quite assumed

Agony in the word "despair"
Of never thinking, looking twice
At the person who was always there
The one who stood by you in life

Wavelengths

Cupid
Daniel S. Janik

Evening...
Little things fly scitter-scatter near lamplights
Birds sleep
Houses close their weary eyelids
Tumbleweeds roll along deserted roads
Quicksilver shadows
The moon's highway.
All the world dreams in expectation
Of another dream

Wavelengths

Fragility
IKO

Fragility of men's spirit
Idleness of his thought
Life built on perceptions of waves
Abstract concepts raising tall structures of beauty

Fragility of men's world built on ideas

Wavelengths

He Stood There Transfixed

Jean Yamasaki Toyama

Pierced with a rope
through his penis.
Shield Jaguar, Mayan king of Yaxchilan
pulls at his pain
for his people.

And again, ecstatic
they believe.

Lady Xoc pulls a rope
through her tongue
and with the blood
writes to the Gods.

Both now only in bas relief,
glyphs I decipher in wonder
translating stone into action
marveling at human desire
making life a meaningful thing.

Inside Myself
Erin L. George

There's only one place to go
so deep inside myself, my soul.
I'll curl up like an infant child,
tucked behind an awkward smile.
In this place there is no judge
(hair knotted twice for love).

Goodbye hatred,
I've got to jet . . .

Once place for me, left to visit -
deep inside myself, my soul.
I'll sleep beneath my wild heart,
counting beats I'd forgot.
In this place there is no hate
(dancing barefoot has its grace).

Goodbye, cruel world
I'll climb inside.
Don't look for me -
I've made up my mind.

There's only one place left to go
deep inside myself, my soul.
I'll play with dreams inside my mind
forgetting, now, to count the time.

The Alcoholic
Alex Kelley

He drinks, and drinks, and drinks....
how much more can he handle?
a different emotion in every glass,
a different time, a different place,
and all the while he still waits for the taste to kick in.

He thinks, and thinks, and thinks....
how much more can he handle?
the lights, the sound, the pleasure, the pain,
they're all slowly becoming more and more of a blur,
how can he stand it? How is he still standing?
and all the while he still waits for the buzz to kick in.

He sinks, and sinks, and sinks...
not much more he can handle,
the voices that surround him,
he's no longer sure where they're coming from,
are they in the room? Are they in his head?
No one knows....
Too many questions float through his head,
but not as much as all of the confusion~
that now floats in his drink....
and all the while he still waits for the good time to kick
in...

Wavelengths

Beyond Beyond
Jean Yamasaki Toyama

I thought myself past passion
beyond caring, outside,
beside myself beyond.

I thought myself past passion
irretrievable, lost
gone down beyond some end
really.

Yes, I was past passion
flat, beyond, out spaced
unlucked and unlived
without suitable end
surfing on self-pity.

Then I saw him, one more luckless than
I, a slob of a self, sprawled on the floor of the mall.

I kicked him absentmindedly thinking he too
wouldn't care. But he rolled toward me full face.
Surprised I gasped. He glared.
And feeble though he was, he rose and stumbled after me.
Alarmed I quickened my step, found reason to run.

Beyond his reach I felt renewed, awakened,
returned from beyond.

Wavelengths

The Subjunctive Mode
IKO

Subjunctive mode,
realm of the unreal,
expression of desire.

It is but your will that makes it indicative.

John-Robert (JR) Coleman is a Hawaiʻi based teacher, published poet/author of the book entitled, "Pearl Drops of Aloha."(www.pearldropsofaloha.com). As an artistic entrepreneur, John-Robert has pioneered and now implements a newly formed inspirational, educational product entitled, "Heart Card Deck: Your Self-Guided Companion to Inner Wisdom and Empowered Relationships." Currently John-Robert manages Heart Card Productions LLC. (www.heartcardproductions.com) and consults by partnering with non-profit agencies and private business to enhance their awareness and fund-raising objectives. He holds a BA in Social Sciences and MPA, Masters in Public Administration in Organizational Development with the California State University, East Bay. He is a member of Toastmasters International and is available for speaking engagements and personal consultations.

Awake!

J.R. Coleman

As for all those lies I bought along the way?Flip them
upside down to right side up,Seeing the truth is in the
undoing~Please, let's stop all payments of spending on
petty illusions and worldly toys.May I peel back the masks
from my imagined idols Arrest this egocentric clatter and
chatter?This noise, this busyness we think all that
matters.Let's invest in seizing the calmThen embrace the
light of love Step out
Raise your lantern
So others may awake
In the power and glory of
The Spirit-in-you!

Penny Lynn Cates grew up in the small hamlet of Hurkett, in Northwestern Ontario, where she resided with her family until she ventured out into the world on her own. With a background in business and commerce and certified in Management Supervising she found her calling in hospital and pharmacy accounting. Seven years ago she relocated to beautiful Georgian Bay, Ontario, with her life companion to enjoy the quiet serenity of cottage country. Currently employed as a sales merchandiser, she still finds time to write poetry and is currently working on her first novel.

The Language of Life
Penny Lynn Cates

Signs and symbols everywhere,
speaking the language of life;
like the white-tailed deer
peering through the living room window,
foretelling the time of plenty is near; or
the blue butterfly that I quickly shooed away,
as it circled about me on an evening walk,
portending sympathy of an upcoming sad day.

As time passes by and events unfold, I recall
the signs and symbols that spoke directly
to Soul, making the connection.

Do I consciously embrace the language of life,
or choose to nod off into a deep comfortable sleep
only to be nudged awake again, the next time my
memory recalls?

Wavelengths

Abandon Piano

J.R. Coleman

Be it my own expectation, my observation
Be it real or imagined, I can't help but to feel, to write you
And this too I pray and candidly say,
Stirring in your heart I believe is a passion that can be
reawakened.
But still I observe there resides within you a lonesome
love,
An untouched love, that asks of itself to be joined here.
This precious gift, a talent you have been given
Perhaps buried, denied or forgotten,
Yet how dear you are to me my friend
For one must share what is natural to one's heart
And so my precious one, come forth and play,
A magnificent love song awaits and is seeking you!
It is as near as your free will, to choose
To renew a love that will always finds its way.
I have dreamt many will come whom thirst to hear you
play
Know you need not fear, for the path is still open and
clear.

Four Arrows, of Cherokee and Irish ancestry, is the author of numerous books, chapters and articles on topics relating to wellness and Indigenous worldviews. Recipient of the Martin Springer Institute on Holocaust Studies Moral Courage Award, he continues his writing and activism while working as a professor of Educational Leadership and Change at Fielding Graduate University.

Dedication

To the man who taught me the importance of each person expressing his or her full potentiality.

My Epitaph
Four Arrows

That I may die upon the morrow,
The probability is high.
And though my love may weep in sorrow,
Still I know that I must try.
That I must try to dare it all
In spite of fear or danger-
That I must answer every call,
So life won't be a stranger.
Oh is it courage that makes me challenge dying?
Or merely the belief that death is timed by fate?
Should I try and keep on trying?
Or merely sleep and eat and wait?
For many life is mere survival,
But I was blessed with strength and wealth
So I must search for the answers vital
For helping bring us back toward health.
So let this poem be my epitaph.
I merely wondered and I tried.
I fought and loved
And laughed and cried,
But while living life
I died!

Wavelengths

The Dancing Stars

Penny Lynn Cates

A young girl walks home
from the outdoor skating rink
with her older brother.
He is in charge. It is his responsibility
to see her home safely after their
evening skate.

He walks briskly ahead of her, without
a care in the world. She quickens her pace to
keep up to him, but to no avail. He walks faster
and faster, testing her abilities; but her pleasures
are few and she loiters behind taking in the beauty
of the full moon and the stars sparkling like
diamonds in the night sky.

She inhales a breath of cold, crisp northwestern
Ontario air; she exhales, mystified by the puff of
breath that lingers behind. Again she looks upward
to the heavens, admiring the beauty that her eyes behold.
A falling star catches her attention and she stands in awe
of the colors displayed as it makes its descent to who
knows where. She makes a wish.

Her brother calls out to her, but she pays no mind.
She has been drawn into the world of wonder, that special
place where she takes refuge from the world. Again she
peeks up
at the night sky and the stars begin to dance, forming all of
her favorite fairy tale characters; Hansel and Gretal, the
Fairy

Godmother, Cinderella, Snow White and the Seven
Dwarfs, and
she knows that God has given her a special message.

The message takes years to decode.

Wavelengths

Time: A Chronological Entity

Alex Kelley

Time is my home.

It's where I sleep.
It's where I wake.
Time is my road.
It's where I started.
It's where I'll end.
Time is my friend,
It keeps me company.
It makes me smile.
Time is my destination.
It's where I've been.
It's where I am.
It's where I'm going.
Time is my currency.
It's what I've earned.
It's what I've saved.
It's what I've spent.
Time is my enemy.
It has deceived me.
It has betrayed me.
Time is my treasure.
I have once lost it.
I have once found it.
Time is everything.
Time is nothing.
Everyone and no one.
Here, there, everywhere....
Yet, nowhere.
As large as the end of all things,

and as small as a watch on a wrist.
A giant set of metal arms on a lit face,
a tiny grain of sand in an oddly shaped glass.
An entity that knows no bounds.
Yet, a prisoner of its own ways...

Nadia Cox is a lawyer, criminologist and poet - she writes to free her emotions and her imagination; to do penance to the thoughts that linger...in a woman's mind. Her works have been published by the South African Institute of Poetry. She lives in South Africa with her family.

Dedication

To my dad, my husband and my beautiful children Reza and Imaad.

Deo Volente

Nadia Cox

On this day, today
I shook hands with destiny.
She tapped me on my back
before turning the rest of me.
Whatever choice you make, she said
 is the one that's meant for you,
the path that will lead you there,
to a place that's meant to be.

This perplexity
Has got me questioning the dexterity of my religion,
it depletes all the air in my soul.
I see your prayers have been answered, Deo volente,
this makes me so foul.
How many Duas will it take before my Islamic life is
turned?
How many Hail Marys must be said before the halo is
burned?

Can I surrender to my God being separated in two?
I think that I shall pray instead
And hope with faith that it will do.

Jason Sturner was born in Harvey, Illinois, and raised in the western suburbs of Chicago. He is a member of the Illinois State Poetry Society and has published three books of poetry: Kairos, 10 Love Poems, and Selected Poems 2004-2007. He resides in Wheaton, Illinois and works as a botanist at the Morton Arboretum in Lisle. Website: www.jasonsturner.blogspot.com

Before the Storm Wet the Earth

Jason Sturner

A ladybug landed on my knee
as I sat alone in a meadow
awaiting the rain.

With its tiny head cocked
and a trust in my silence
it seemed to ask,

"Do you think I am beautiful?"

But all I could do
was look away
and wonder what stories
my face was telling.

Wavelengths

Words Like Burning Coals

Jean Yamasaki Toyama

He hurled them at her
unspeakable names
that scorched their way through
and sank in her belly, where they lay
searing and sputtering until
one day she turned
salamander.

Then she stoked herself with
kiawe driftwood, talapia heads,
boar tusks, oil slicks:
everything. All swirled
under fire, spiraled within,
a galaxy of sidereal desire.

Wavelengths

Pathway
Daniel S. Janik

There is a still place for us
Somewhere inside the yellow of daffodil petals
Somewhere inside the marshmallow-white of sea foam
Though you exist these days only in the midnight depths
of occasional thunder,
Shudders of sky-spine,
Tosses of warm, summer rain-hair,
Flickers of cool, Japanese wind-eyes.
Your eyes these days are in faraway lands,
On faraway places,
Not on me
Yet I feel your presence pervade
Every caterpillar hair, Every drop of perspiration
Between thighs, lips, thoughts, eyes.
It is as if I raped the essence of everything living,
To experience the excelsior heights of being,
To unfold and extend off of my physical body
Over the pathway to the distant, evening star.

Converging
Nadia Cox

This profound yearning
Diffuses the winter in our African sky
Beget trickling streams of passionate sweat, spent
On supple flesh, throbbing and proud
A nakedness that lingers no more, an essence set free in
bliss
We are the forbidden fruit

Here is our garden
Covetous no longer
Our selves are interlinking pieces of this beautiful oracle
the remnants of what has passed
the mélange of what is now
Tousled hair and mangled bodies
Contortions of orgasm etched into our faces

Resting eyes release a sigh of pleasure
Skin still moist and scented
Washed by the passion of our own paradise
Two hearts dancing to the rhythm of the djembe,
two solitudes singing our song
And so we remain

Wavelengths

If

Erin L George

If I was there with you tonight,
we'd paint the town the deepest crimson -
making memories out of pocket change
and stirring up the gods.

A tornado would mate
with a hurricane
and baby horeshoe crabs
would wash ashore.

If I was in your arms tonight
I'd squeeze you so tight the blood
would rush to your head
and you'd beg me to stop.

The ghetto would take a bow
and curtsey just before
tucking a napkin in its collar
and lighting a candle.

If you were by my side tonight,
we'd love hard enough
to make the neighbors blush with their
cups pressed to the wall.

The city would blink twice
and traffic would stop
to watch us cross sidewalks
on the lower East Side.

Wavelengths

Fresh Morning
Jason Sturner

Talk to me in the comfort of fresh morning
when a bird's song I may enjoy
as the cold of night surrenders to the warmth of dawn
and there comes no sound from the telephone or door.

Hold me close as the sun plays with shadows
when the curtains of our room blow wide
as our hearts beat ever so quietly to the pulse of day
and seagulls scavenge across the falling tide.

Know me when the day is newly born, my love
when the spirit within this aging body is content
as I steal gentle kisses from your soft lips
and inhale the subtle fragrance of this moment.

Bella Vista

Nadia Cox

The papayas have been eaten,
two boxes in two days.
Three apples remain, supposedly bruised.
I can't wait to come by again.

It's Tuesday.
I was there yesterday.
Perhaps, on Friday we could make a date?
Talk about the weather; the sweetness of the melons and
the differences between the Navels and the Valencias.
Don't forget the eel worms in the strawberries.

Time passed by playful, blissful.
When I get home, I realize I've forgotten the bananas.
I can't wait to come by again.

Morning Rain

Jason Sturner

This morning there was much rain,
forcing the birds into trees,
the butterflies beneath leaves.

I stand at the open window,
listening for the cool silence
between raindrops.

I begin to wonder
about time machines,
about being fully absorbed into the future:

> The full view of a sunset
> from our porch chairs,
> a cat resting at our feet.
> Faces aged, a hand
> holding a hand.

> And the wind
> comes down from flowered hills,
> filling the home with fragrances.
> Everything is golden orange
> like a softly glowing jewel.

I blink and turn from the window.
Another routine day begins.
The echoes of my heartbeat
will mingle with the rain.

Wavelengths

In Communion

Jeremy Ussher

All of my senses overtaken by the rugged landscape, so
majestic and bold.
Raucous winds pull the storm upon me. And, the
trees sway. They
dance the familiar rain-dance of their ancestors.
Familiar, but evolved.
Birthed in ice, they howl a song that brings the snow.
Their roots spiral,
boring deeper into the granite boulders. They have
dedicated a lifetime to split and hold,
disregarding mass,
penetrating stone and earth unseen...or
is it?

Now, my eyes are set upon the water.
Its unruly surface masks the depth of color with waves and
whitecaps.
What treasures must lie below,
forsaken gifts of unknown circumstances,
impossible answers to seemingly irrelevant questions
two worlds separate, yet so reliant.
So, I say "thank You."

More than nourishment, I need.
More than beauty, I need.
More than fulfillment, I need.
More than existence, I need.

Here I am on this rock,
awaiting the inevitable storm,

listening to the trees,
acknowledging the mysteries of the water,
loving all that I have been given today.
Suddenly, I don't need anything.
Now, I have got it all.

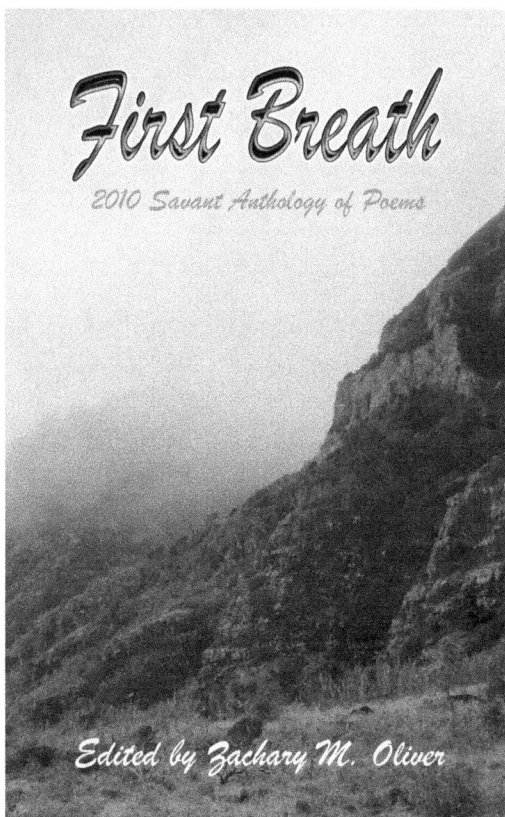

If you enjoyed *Wavelengths: 2011 Savant Anthology of Poems*, consider the first in the series, *First Breath: 2010 Savant Anthology of Poems*

Twenty-nine poems by ten outstanding poets and writers selected for their outstanding merit including Helen Doan, Erin L. George, Jack Howard, Daniel S. Janik, Scott Mastro, Zachary M. Oliver, Francis H. Powell, Gabjirel Ra, V. Bright Saigal and Orest Stocco

First Breath (2010) edited by Zachary M. Oliver
from Savant Books and Publications

If you enjoyed *Wavelengths: 2011 Savant Anthology of Poems* consider these other fine Books from Savant Books and Publications:

Other Savant Poetry Books by These Authors:

First Breath Edited by Zachary M. Oliver
Last and Final Harvest by Daniel S. Janik
The Illustrated Middle Earth by Daniel S. Janik
Footprints, Smiles and Little White Lies by Daniel S. Janik

Other Savant Books by These Poets:

A Whale's Tale by Daniel S. Janik
Falling but Fulfilled by Zachary M. Oliver
Last Song of the Whales by Four Arrows
On My Behalf by Helen Doan

Other Outstanding Savant Books:

Ammon's Horn by Guerrino Amati

Who's Killing All the Lawyers? by A. G. Hayes

Kim Chan by Ilan Herman

Wretched Land by Mila Komarnisky

In Dire Straits by Jim Currie

My Two Wives and Three Husbands by S. Stanley Gordon

Number One Bestseller by Brian Morley

Charlie No Face by David B. Seaburn

Richer by Jean Blasiar

Hello, Norma Jean by Sue Dolleris

Mythical Voyage by Robin Ymer

Manifest Intent by Mike Farris

Perilous Panacea by Ronald Klueh

My Unborn Child by Orest Stocco

William Maltese's Flicker by William Maltese

The Jumper Chronicles by W. C. Peever

Poor Rich by Jean Blasiar

Kanaka Blues by Mike Farris

Called Home by Gloria Schumann

The Bahrain Conspiracy by Bentley Gates

Today I Am A Man by Larry Rodness

Dare to Love in Oz by William Maltese

The Village Curtain by Tony Tame

Tropic of California by R. Page Kaufman

Savant Books Scheduled for Release in 2011:

Blood Money by Scott Mastro
In the Himalayan Nights by Anoop Chandola
Random Views of Asia by William Sharp
Almost Paradise by Laurie Hanan

www.ingramcontent.com/pod-product-compliance
Lightning Source LLC
Chambersburg PA
CBHW060130050426
42448CB00010B/2046